THE ULTIMATE PROFIT BOOSTER

Over 100 profit boosting techniques for your business

by F. John Morine

HUTCHINSON BUSINESS
London Melbourne Auckland Johannesburg

Hutchinson Business
An imprint of Century Hutchinson Ltd
62–65 Chandos Place, London WC2N 4NW

Century Hutchinson Australia Pty Ltd
16–22 Church Street, Hawthorn, Melbourne, Victoria 3122

Century Hutchinson Group (NZ) Ltd
32–34 View Road, PO Box 40–086, Glenfield, Auckland 10

Century Hutchinson Group (SA) Pty Ltd
PO Box 337, Bergvlei 2012, South Africa

First published in New Zealand, 1980, by Managerial Publications
under the title *Bigger Profits in the 80's*
First UK edition, 1981, published by Business Books
under the title *Riding the Recession*

Reprinted 1987

Printed and bound in Great Britain by
The Guernsey Press Co. Ltd., Guernsey, Channel Islands.

British Library Cataloguing in Publication Data

Morine, F. John
  (Bigger profits in the 80s). The ultimate
  profit-booster.
  1. Business enterprises – Finance
  I. Title II. The ultimate profit-booster
  III. Morine, F. John. Riding the recession
  658.1'5   HG4026

ISBN 0 09 159201 1 paper

ISBN 0 09 172811 8 cased

CONTENTS

Chapter   **Page**

Objective   vii

PART A: ACTION NOW

1   Three routes to profit growth   3

2   Small improvements can raise profit substantially   11

3   Identify key areas for action   17

4   Establish your initial profit plan   23

5   Plan cash flow   27

PART B: MARKETING FOR MORE PROFIT

6   What is your unique selling proposition?   33

7   Basic research to raise sales   39

8   Avoid the perils of higher volume/low margin business   47

9   Know your product costs   51

10 Raise the productivity of sales staff   53

11 Pursue further opportunities for growth   61

12 Deleting products can raise profit   67

13 Pricing for profit   71

14 How to advertise — and get results   77

PART C: REDUCING COSTS

15 Key aspects of cost reduction 87

16 Manage your time for profit 95

17 Raise productivity through people 101

18 Achieve peak efficiency in purchasing and stock control 109

19 Are you minimising taxation? 119

20 Critically examine your information system 123

21 Speed up collections from debtors 127

22 Put non-productive assets to work 135

23 Reduce other costs 139

PART D: IMPLEMENTING CHANGES

24 Get commitment to profit improvement 145

25 Monitor progress and take corrective action 151

26 Plan longer term strategy 155

Afterword 159

Note: Until a suitable unisex pronoun is introduced the reader should read 'he' or 'she' as preferred.

OBJECTIVE

The objective of this book is to present and explain practical, down-to-earth techniques you can use NOW to increase the profits of your business.

Particular attention is given to immediate ways of:

1   Raising the volume of sales, your competitive advantage and profit margins.

2   Ensuring that you keep your finger on the pulse of the key areas of your business.

Businessmen, entrepreneurs, owners and managers are dedicated to growth. Growth means expansion, more sales, bigger profits and higher returns on investment.

However, as we proceed through the 1980s, the business environment has changed. Those businesses which have emerged from the recession, having faced shrinking markets, high inflation and rising costs, are leaner and more wary. Growth must now be profitable growth.

Opportunities for profitable growth

Business has been through a testing time. The opportunities for profitable growth are there for those businesses willing to *compete aggressively with imagination and commitment to their profit objectives.*

These key qualities imply a need to search rigorously for creative ways of exploiting marketing opportunities and fresh approaches for resolving problems. In short, profitable strategies for out-performing competitors. This book examines a wide range of such strategies.

For managers under pressure

I have structured this book to meet the needs of busy managers working under pressure.

1   Extensive use is made of checklists to enable you to grasp points quickly.

2   Space is provided at the end of each chapter for you to make your notes on particular items for action in your business.

Select relevant ideas

Not all ideas are applicable to every business. Some will be particularly relevant in one situation, others in another. Select for implementation those ideas you judge to be most relevant to your firm's specific needs. Do implement them!

To survive and be successful in business you must make a profit — a real profit not a paper one — and make it NOW!

Part A

ACTION NOW

Chapter 1

THREE ROUTES TO PROFIT GROWTH

In any business there are three possible ways to improve profit. These are:

1. Increase sales volume

2. Raise selling prices

3. Reduce costs.

If the outputs of your business are services rather than physical products, the foregoing can be modified and restated as:

1. Increase the quantity of services provided[1].

2. Raise unit charges. For example, hourly fee rates or commission rates.

3. Reduce costs.

Alternative terms

Sometimes managers use more sophisticated terms than these. For example, they may refer to:

— Changing the product mix.

— Altering the gross profit mix of the product range.

— Changing the customer mix.

But each of these are variations of the three basic strategies stated above.

Why not lower prices?

Today's stagnant or shrinking markets are characterised by intense competition. Many firms operating in these markets are endeavouring to maintain or increase their sales volumes by lowering their selling prices 'to meet the competition'. And in turn this reduces the gross margin on each product sold.

The rationale behind lowering selling prices is that hopefully this move will enable the firm to secure an increase in sales volume such that the lower gross profit obtained on each unit sold will be more than offset by the higher aggregate amount of gross profit achieved.

[1]The term 'products' as used in this book refers to the end outputs of your business. It includes both physical products and service offerings.

For example, in Figure 1 the first column shows a profit plan (or operating budget) for the ABC Company for one year assuming a selling price of £10.00 per unit sold.[1] The second column is an alternative plan showing what management hopes to achieve for the same year, but with the selling price per unit reduced by 10% to £9.00 'to meet the competition'.

FIGURE 1

ABC Company Ltd

Alternative profit plans for one year

	Profit plan based on a selling price of £10 per unit	Alternative plan with selling price reduced to £9 per unit
	£	£
SALES		
50,000 units @ £10.00 each	500,000	
65,000 units @ £9.00 each		585,000
Less direct costs		
£5.00 per unit	250,000	325,000
GROSS TRADING PROFIT	250,000	260,000
Less indirect costs		
Administration, financial, selling and distribution		
costs	200,000	200,000
NET PROFIT BEFORE TAXATION	£50,000	£60,000

[1] If your firm's output consists of service products rather than physical products, Figure 1 and subsequent illustrations can be reworked to demonstrate the points being made with items and poundamounts relevant in your circumstances.

In practice however, the strategy of lowering selling prices is fraught with the following dangers:

1. Little volume increase

In an intensely competitive market situation it is most likely that competitors are also reducing their selling prices. That is, a price war is in progress. Accordingly, instead of increasing sales by 15,000 units as in the second column of Figure 1, it is probable the ABC Company will achieve little if any increase in volume as a result of reducing its prices by 10%.

2. Indirect costs increase

In Figure 1 it is assumed that indirect costs will remain constant at $200,000 when sales volume increases by 15,000 units. In practice however, an increase in volume can rarely be achieved without a greater input of indirect costs. This is particularly so in a highly competitive market. For example, extra expenditure will be required on items such as advertising and other promotion costs, salesmen's remuneration and distribution costs.

These projected factors have been built into Figure 2 where it is assumed that the following events would occur if the firm reduced its selling prices by 10%:

1. Sales volume would rise by 4% from 50,000 to 52,000 units.

2. Indirect costs would rise by 5% from £200,000 to £210,000 as a result of the greater input required to achieve the 4% increase in sales volume in the highly competitive market in which the ABC Company operates.

The figures in the second column of Figure 2 are indicative of the disastrous results of a firm which reduces selling prices in a bid to increase sales volume, while operating in a highly competitive market.

FIGURE 2

ABC Company Ltd

Comparison of actual results for one year allowing for projected factors

	Actual results based on a selling price of £10 per unit	Actual results if selling prices had been reduced by 10%
	£	£
SALES		
50,000 units @ £10.00 each	500,000	
52,000 units @ £9.00 each		468,000
Less direct costs		
£5.00 per unit	250,000	260,000
GROSS TRADING PROFIT	250,000	208,000
Less indirect costs		
Administration, financial, selling and distribution costs	200,000	210,000
NET PROFIT/(LOSS) BEFORE TAXATION	£50,000	£(2,000)

Further problems caused by inflation

At this point we need to also consider the further complications caused by inflation. In a high inflation situation both the direct and indirect costs of the ABC Company (as shown in Figures 1 and 2) will typically be increasing. These increased costs can be financed from two possible sources, namely:

1. Net profits earned by the firm, or

2. Outside borrowings.

But as demonstrated in the second column of Figure 2, lowering selling prices in a competitive market situation reduces net profit. (In fact Figure 2 shows that the ABC Company would have made a net loss of £2,000 if prices had been reduced by 10%). In these circumstances the ABC Company would need to borrow more funds from outside sources to finance increases in operating costs incurred in the year following the period dealt with in Figure 2.

If the firm again reduces selling prices in that following year 'to meet the competition' this precipitates a vicious circle thus:

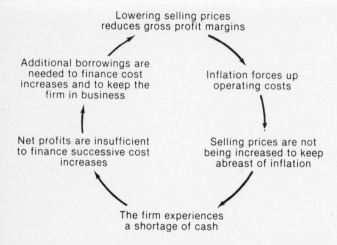

A business which attempts to maintain or increase volume by reducing selling prices in an intensely competitive/high inflation situation may suddenly find it has little if any net profit remaining.

Further dangerous aspects of a strategy aimed at higher volumes at the expense of profit margins are dealt with in Chapter 8.

Alternatives to lowering prices

Subsequent chapters explain numerous alternative methods you can use to raise the net profit of your business. These techniques all fall within the parameters of the three major routes to profit growth discussed at the outset, namely:

1. Increase sales volume

2. Raise selling prices

3. Reduce costs.

ITEMS FOR ACTION NOW

Chapter 2

SMALL IMPROVEMENTS CAN RAISE PROFIT SUBSTANTIALLY

Most firms require only moderate increases in sales volume or selling prices or moderate decreases in costs, to obtain substantial increases in net profit. This point is demonstrated in Figure 3.

Assume that the first draft of the ABC Company's profit plan for a particular year is summarised in the column on the immediate left of Figure 3. Management is not satisfied with this profit plan and wishes to increase net profit for this year by 50% — quite a substantial increase.

FIGURE 3

ABC Company Ltd

How net profit can be lifted by 50% by changes in sales volume, selling prices or costs

First draft of profit plan		Increase sales volume by 10%	OR raise selling prices by 5%	OR reduce direct costs by 10%	OR reduce indirect costs by 12½%
£		£	£	£	£
500,000	SALES	550,000	525,000	500,000	500,000
250,000	Less direct costs	275,000	250,000	225,000	250,000
250,000	GROSS TRADING PROFIT	275,000	275,000	275,000	250,000
200,000	Less indirect costs	200,000	200,000	200,000	175,000
£50,000	NET PROFIT BEFORE TAX	£75,000	75,000	75,000	75,000

As shown in Figure 3 this objective can be achieved by either:

1. Increasing sales volume by 10% (assuming no increase in indirect costs in handling the extra volume); or

2. Raising selling prices by 5%; or

3. Reducing direct costs by 10%; or

4. Reducing indirect costs by 12½%.

Examine your alternatives

You can construct the equivalent of Figure 3 for your firm, examining a range of alternative ways in which you can deliberately alter volumes, prices and costs to lift net profit by the amount you require.

It should be noted that Figure 3 is not intended to imply that raising net profit by a substantial amount can be accomplished easily. Each of the four alternative methods illustrated in Figure 3 requires dedicated commitment and hard work. However, the purpose of Figure 3 is to demonstrate the alternatives available for raising net profit.

Advantages of raising prices

In an exercise such as this it is typical to find that a small increase in selling prices has a dramatic effect in lifting net profit, provided sales volume does not drop as a result of the price increase. This is the case in Figure 3 where an increase of 5% in selling prices produces a 50% increase in net profit.

The advantages of raising selling prices as a means of achieving profit growth are:

1. **Quicker return**

   A price increase is typically the fastest way to increase profit. Assuming that sales do not drop away, additional profit accrues immediately the price change becomes effective.

   By contrast it usually takes considerably more time to increase sales volume, especially in a highly competitive market.

2. **Less time and effort**

   The time and effort needed to make a price change is typically less than is required to increase sales volume or reduce costs.

Later chapters and chapter 13 in particular, will deal with the question of how to raise prices without suffering a drop in the volume of business transacted.

Effect of cumulative improvements

So far we have considered changes in sales volume, prices and costs independently of each other. But if small improvements are made in each of these areas at the same time, the cumulative effect of these improvements on net profit can be substantial. This principle is demonstrated in Figure 4.

FIGURE 4

ABC Company Ltd

The effect on net profit of small, combined improvements in sales volume, prices and costs

First draft of profit plan		With a 2% increase in sales volume	Followed by a rise in selling prices of 2%	Followed by a 2% reduction in total costs
£		£	£	£
500,000	SALES	510,000	520,200	520,200
250,000	Less direct costs	255,000	255,000	249,900
250,000	GROSS TRADING PROFIT	255,000	265,200	270,300
200,000	Less indirect costs	200,000	200,000	196,000
£50,000	NET PROFIT BEFORE TAX	£55,000	65,200	74,300

In Figure 4 the ABC Company has increased sales volume by 2%, raised prices by 2% and reduced overall costs by 2%.

Although each of these percentage changes are small, their cumulative effect is to lift net profit by a substantial 49% from £50,000 to £74,300.

Your alternatives for profit growth

Again, you can construct the equivalent of Figure 4 for your business to examine the overall growth in net profit which could be achieved from small improvements in volume, prices and costs.

ITEMS FOR ACTION NOW

Chapter 3

IDENTIFY KEY AREAS FOR ACTION

The most common source of mistakes in management decisions is the emphasis on finding the right answer, rather than the right question.

— Peter Drucker

You may consider you know your firm's strengths (what you do best) and weaknesses (problem areas) so well that you are already aware of those key areas requiring urgent improvements to boost profit and cash flow.

However, before taking action it is wise to diagnose your firm's recent operating performance and financial position. The purpose of this exercise is to ascertain (or confirm) those key areas in which profit improvement effort should be concentrated to obtain maximum effect.

Operating results

Schedule out your firm's operating results in columnar form for each of the past five years as the basis for examining the following:

1. **Sales (or gross income)**

   (a) Adjust for price increases each year to ascertain real increases or decreases in volume of business from year to year.

   (b) Analyse sales by appropriate dimensions such as products, product groups, customers or market segments, as the basis for ascertaining:

   — Which 20% of your products are responsible for 80% of total sales dollars?

   — Which 20% of your customers account for 80% of total sales?[1]

---

[1] Here we have two examples of Pareto's Law, otherwise known as the 80/20 rule. This states that 20% of the causes in any situation will produce 80% of the results — or figures roughly similar to these. The important point about Pareto's Law is that it shows where to concentrate your efforts: on the 20% of causes which have the greatest effect. Other examples of the application of Pareto's Law appear in later chapters.

2. **Operating costs**

Examine the relationship (percentage) of key expense items to sales.

3. **Gross profit and net profit**

Examine the relationship (percentage) of gross profit to sales and net profit to sales.

4. **Product margins**

Plot product margins for each product or product group if these are known.

5. **Sales order backlog**

Compare this indicator at intervals over the five year period under review.

6. **Stock turn**

Calculate and compare the rate of stock turnover for each year. The formula for this calculation is:

$$\frac{\text{Cost of sales}}{\text{Average of (opening stock + closing stock)}}$$

7. **Closing stock/sales**

Examine the relationship (percentage) of closing stock to sales for each year.

Trends in each of the above indicators should be examined over the past five years to reveal:

1. Where your firm's strengths lie; and

2. Problem areas for immediate action. For example, does the above analysis indicate that sales volumes are declining, product margins are shrinking or certain cost items are rising at unacceptable rates?

It could also be particularly useful to compare the above indicators with those of other firms in your industry, if this information is available for the period under review.

Financial position

Calculate and examine trends in the following indicators as at balance sheet date for each of the past five years:

1. **Debtors**

    The average period of credit granted to debtors. The formula for this calculation is:

    $$\frac{\text{Debtors}}{\text{Average daily credit sales}}$$

2. **Debt ratio**

    The formula for calculating the debt ratio (or measure of capital gearing) is:

    $$\frac{\text{Current liabilities} + \text{long term liabilities}}{\text{Total tangible assets}}$$

    expressed as a percentage.

3. Return on investment

This is the most important indicator of all as it is the overall measure of business profitability or performance. The precise indicator used here may vary with circumstances, but the usual measure adopted for a company is:

$$\frac{\text{Net profit after taxation}}{\text{Shareholders' funds}}$$

expressed as a percentage. [1]

The foregoing analyses of operating results and financial position will reveal **what** has happened during the period under review. The next important step is to ascertain the major reasons **why** favourable and adverse trends have developed in the business with a view to:

1. Reinforcing favourable features (strengths); and

2. Rectifying adverse features (weaknesses).

Subsequent chapters suggest typical reasons for adverse trends and a variety of ways in which these may be tackled and corrected.

[1] Clearly alternative measures of business performance would apply in the case of a sole proprietor or partnership. For example, 'net profit before taxation' may be the most appropriate measure in the latter cases.

ITEMS FOR ACTION NOW

Chapter 4

ESTABLISH YOUR INITIAL PROFIT PLAN

A recently overheard comment by one businessman to another:

'We are a non-profit organisation. We didn't plan it that way, but that's the way it worked out'.

At this point it is important to establish a profit plan (or operating budget) for the current financial year if one does not already exist, so that you know where your business is heading.

The following points should be borne in mind when constructing the profit plan:

1. Net profit objective

At the outset careful consideration should be given to the amount of 'net profit after tax' required for the year. Due account should be taken of the need to cover the following items:

(a) The amount by which the owners' equity invested in the business will be eroded by inflation during the year.

If this question of maintaining the purchasing power of owners' funds is not taken into account, the chances are there may be no 'real' profit achieved for the year after allowing for this factor.

(b) Dividend payments to shareholders or other appropriate returns to the owners of the business.

(c) The need to finance asset replacements including any increases in debtors and stocks.

2. Sharpening up the profit plan

Typically the first draft of the profit plan will show a net profit figure which falls short of the objective in 1. above. The task is then to 'bridge the gap' so the desired profit will be achieved.

In this regard:

(a) Allowance should be made for planned improvements in sales and costs arising from the company diagnosis described in Chapter 3.

(b) Each manager should be clearly accountable for specific revenue and/or cost items in line with the principle of 'managerial accountability'.

(c) Each manager should be required to rigorously 'cost justify' each item of expense for which he is accountable. This approach should be clearly distinguished from the traditional approach to budgeting often used in the past, namely, 'taking last year's figure for each expense item and adding on a percentage to cover this year's inflation'.

3. Further improvements

Your profit plan will be subject to later modifications as the result of selecting and implementing ideas for profit improvement from the chapters following.

ITEMS FOR ACTION NOW

Chapter 5

PLAN
CASH FLOW

It is also vital to construct a cash flow plan (or cash budget) for
the current financial year. In a period of stagnant or declining
markets and high inflation a firm may show a 'paper' profit, but
this surplus can be rapidly eroded in financing rising costs, including increased amounts required for debtors and stocks.

In this situation ensuring that the firm will continue to have adequate cash resources is clearly of crucial importance. Hence the
cash flow plan.

Recommended format

A recommended format for the cash flow plan on a monthly basis is shown in Figure 5.

FIGURE 5

	JANUARY		FEBRUARY		
ABC Company Ltd					
Cash flow plan for the year ending 31 December 19..					
	Plan	Actual	Plan	Actual	
	£	£	£	£	
Opening balance/overdraft					
Cash receipts					
Receipts from debtors					
Cash sales					
Other income					
Proceeds from sale of plant					
Total cash receipts					
Cash payments					
Purchases					
Salaries and wages					
Vehicle expenses					
Other expenses (itemised)					
Purchase of vehicle					
Loan repayments					
Taxation					
Total cash payments					
Closing balance/overdraft					

Later modifications

As in the case of the profit plan, the cash flow plan will be subject to later modifications as a result of implementing measures
for profit improvement selected from the chapters following.

Actual results versus the plan

A plan is worthless unless actual progress is plotted against the
plan at regular intervals to ensure the business is on target. Accordingly provision is made in Figure 5 for inserting actual
figures on a monthly basis.

Communicating with your banker

Maintaining good communication with your banker is a sound
policy to follow at all times. However, this principle assumes particular importance in times of tight liquidity.

Submitting copies of your profit plan and cash flow plan to your
bank manager should enhance his confidence in the way you are
managing your business and in particular, the concerted efforts
you are making to improve profit and cash flow.

ITEMS FOR ACTION NOW

Part B

MARKETING FOR MORE PROFIT

Chapter 6

WHAT IS YOUR UNIQUE SELLING PROPOSITION?

People buy only benefits.

A customer is interested only in what a product will do for him. That is, he applies the 'what's in it for me?' yardstick in his buying decisions.

Now consider this question carefully:

Why should customers buy from your firm rather than your competitors?

If a customer's primary concern is the particular benefit a product offers him and you wish to raise your firm's sales volumes, the implication is that it is crucial to know what **particular** benefit a customer is seeking when making his buying decision. Then to give this benefit to him. In other words, to offer him **a unique selling proposition.**

Furthermore, the chances are your competitors have not approached this matter thoroughly. Accordingly in offering customers the benefits they are seeking, you are also ensuring that your firm stands out clearly from your competitors. If it does not, customers are just as likely to buy elsewhere.

The dangers of offering lower prices as a benefit to customers have already been stressed in Chapter 1 and are dealt with again in Chapter 8. Yet in today's intensely competitive markets many firms are ignoring the perils of driving for increased volumes at the expense of profit margins as they continually discount the prices of their products as an inducement for customers to buy.

The desirable alternative then, is to identify a particular benefit or benefits you can offer customers, other than a discounted price. Some examples are:

1. Prompt, courteous and reliable service in a total sense.

2. A convenience feature of the product.

3. A safety feature of the product.

4. Speedy delivery service.

5. A time-saving product feature.

6. Excellent product knowledge and technical know-how.

7. Reliable after-sales service and back-up.

8. An asthetic feature of the product.

9. Taste appeal.

10. A particular benefit in the location of your business.

11. Status appeal of a product.

12. An outstandingly attractive and pleasant shopping environment in a retail business.

13. A unique functional feature of a product.

The particular benefit you offer may vary as between products and customer groups. But the principles remain:

1. To drive up volume and outperform your competitors you must offer customers a unique selling proposition.

2. This proposition must take the form of emphasising a particular benefit(s) accruing to customers who buy your product(s).

3. Emphasising a benefit means not only stressing that particular customer benefit by way of advertising, but also backing up your claim by actually giving that benefit to customers when transacting business with them.

4. Accordingly it is vital that not only sales staff but **all** staff should know clearly what unique selling proposition(s) your firm is offering customers. **Every employee in your firm should work constantly to strengthen that proposition(s).**

Part of the answer in deciding which particular benefit to emphasise in your marketing effort lies in basic and sound market research. In its simplest yet most meaningful form, this means talking to actual and potential customers to ascertain the key factor (or benefit) which influences their buying decisions. This exercise may also disclose why customers prefer a competitor's product, in which case appropriate steps can be taken to rectify your firm's weakness.

Continuously seeking this information is a vital part of the work of a competent sales person.

A further important point to bear in mind is that if you wish to increase your volume of business in a stagnant or shrinking market, this can be achieved only at the expense of competitors. To win a customer away from a competitor can usually be done only by giving that customer **a very good reason** why he should change his buying behaviour.

In the mind of the customer a 'very good reason' will consist of a meaningful benefit accruing to him on switching his patronage to your firm. In the absence of this benefit there is no incentive for the customer to move away from his existing supplier.

A firm which is a true market leader aims at creating an image of 'distinctive professionalism' in its particular industry. Distinctive professionalism in marketing means first and foremost emphasising unique customer benefits for those who buy from that firm. Through the resulting increase in its volume of business the firm benefits at the expense of its competitors.

Dedicated commitment to the principles explained in this chapter will prove to be critical to the continuing survival and profitability of your business in the 1980's.

ITEMS FOR ACTION NOW

Chapter 7

BASIC RESEARCH TO RAISE SALES

Basic market research aimed at providing information to assist you to raise sales volumes can be profitably undertaken in two broad areas:

1. Research based on internal information already available within your business.

2. Research based on information from sources outside your firm.

Each of these two areas are examined in further detail below.

Research based on internal information

Consider the following points which may reveal opportunities to increase volumes in your business:

1. **Sales analysis by customer**

    Have you analysed sales by customer for the current year and compared the volumes purchased by each customer with those of previous years?

    Does this indicate that some customers are being 'under-sold' in the current year, offering potential for further repeat business?

2. **Alternative approach to sales analysis**

    A modified form of the above approach is to identify which 20% of your customers account for 80% of your total sales. Does this suggest potential for further repeat business:

    (a) By selling more to those key customers in the 20% group?

    (b) By selling more to the 80% of customers who are buying low volumes?

3. **Identify all potential customers**

    Are you selling to all those potential customers who could be buyers for your products:

    (a) Within the market segments in which you are presently selling?

    (b) In new market segments, including export markets?

4. **The few customers/few products dilemma**

(a) If you are selling to a small number of customers have you considered what the likely effect would be on your sales and net profit if you lost one key customer?

What actions are you taking to reduce your firm's vulnerability here?

(b) If you sell only one product or a small group of related products have you considered the possible effect on your sales and net profit of a sharp downturn in demand due for example, to a change in technology or the emergence of a powerful new competitor?

Again, what actions are you taking to reduce your firm's vulnerability to such events?

Particular vigilance is needed in each of the foregoing situations. Ideas put forward in the various chapters on marketing in this publication should be helpful in suggesting ways of fortifying your firm if the above factors are relevant.

5. **Conflict between sales and other departments**

(a) Is there any conflict in your business between

(i) The production or purchasing department on the one hand, and

(ii) The sales department on the other

whereby production or purchasing is failing to provide the appropriate mix of products required by the sales department to best meet customer demands?

(b) Do your staffs in these departments meet with each other regularly to discuss ideas and to resolve problems?

The benefits arising from these meetings can be very substantial indeed.

6. Concentrating on higher margin business

Would your firm experience a lift in profit if you adopted a deliberate policy of:

(a) Focussing on those particular products and/or segments of the market where higher margin business could be obtained, and

(b) Retrenching out of those products and/or segments of the market where low margins prevail?

Research based on external information

The following points may also reveal opportunities to increase your volume of business:

1. Total market demand versus supply

Have you undertaken a study to compare:

(a) Total market demand in your industry (both present and future) with

(b) The total productive capacity of suppliers operating in the industry

to assess the degree to which the market may be over or under supplied?

What do your findings suggest concerning the degree of current and future competitiveness in the industry?

2. Trends in market size

Is the total size of the market in which you operate growing, stagnating or shrinking?

Do you know whether this is due to:

(a) The total number of customers increasing or decreasing; or

(b) Volume of sales per customer increasing or decreasing; or

(c) A combination of (a) and (b) above?

What are the implications of your findings for the future of your business?

3. Competitors

How much do you know about your competitor's strengths and weaknesses? In particular:

(a) Could you capitalise on weaknesses in your competitors' marketing practices?

(b) Could you copy selected strengths of your competitors, but outperform them by perfecting these strengths?

4. Keeping in touch with the market

Does your marketing manager make a policy of **personally** keeping in touch with customers and trends in the markets in which your firm operates?

5. Feedback from customers

Do you make a policy of meeting with customers to hear at first hand their views on matters such as:

(a) How you can improve your products and the services your firm provides, thereby securing a larger portion of their business?

(b) Critical factors (benefits) which influence their decisions to buy from your firm or from other suppliers?

(c) Any problems the customer is experiencing with your firm's performance. For example: late deliveries, supplying the customer with the wrong product for his particular needs, off-handed treatment of customers by sales staff — or other aspects of your business which customers may object to.

Of course immediate action should be taken to rectify these problems, otherwise your customer base will be eroded and volumes will fall away.

In this context it is worth remembering that the customer is king. It is he or she who makes the buying decision and therefore, has the final word. **No matter what you may think of your business it is the customer's perception of your firm that is most important.**

ITEMS FOR ACTION NOW

Chapter 8

AVOID THE PERILS OF HIGHER VOLUME/LOW MARGIN BUSINESS

The dangers of lowering selling prices in a competitive market situation in a bid to maintain or increase volumes have already been emphasised.

The perils of adopting a policy aimed at higher volume/low margin business are so real in a declining market/high inflation environment that this topic deserves further elaboration here.

The following additional points should be noted:

1. **Overriding importance of margins**

   Margins are more important than volume when a firm is faced with a stagnant or declining market on the one hand and rising costs on the other. In this situation a firm attempting to maintain or increase volume by cutting margins may suddenly find it has little if any, margins remaining.

2. **A severe cutback is sometimes needed**

   If the company diagnosis recommended in Chapter 3 discloses that much of the business recently acquired by your firm is low margin business, the chances are your firm now faces a critical shortage of cash.

   To correct this situation and ensure the firm's survival it may be necessary to severely cut back low margin business to the point where the firm is operating from a sounder base of lower volume but higher margin business. That is, the firm is retrenched back to a profitable core of higher margin sales.

3. **The income gearing problem**

   A firm aiming to increase sales volume will typically require additional funds to pay for those increases in operating costs necessary to support the increase in business. For example, increases in advertising, selling and distribution costs. If the firm sells on credit and carries stocks it will also require additional cash to finance the increase in debtors and stocks which typically occur with an increase in business. These additional funds usually come from outside borrowings.

   If in addition to these factors the firm is sacrificing profit margins in its drive to expand volumes, then the income gearing of the firm (that is, the amount of interest on borrowings in relation to net profit) will rise.

   No business can allow its income gearing to deteriorate for long without arousing the suspicions of its banker. And in turn the bank's loss of confidence in the firm will ultimately lead to a reluctance to extend further credit.

4. **Avoid profitless growth**

Clearly then, it is vital to avoid profitless growth or 'growth for growth's sake'. Yet it is surprising that many businessmen still deliberately seek to increase sales and their share of the market, with scant regard for margins and net profit.

Setting ambitious and challenging targets in terms of sales and market share is a common enough practice. But in the hands of managers who do not understand the need to set equally ambitious targets for margins and net profit, this policy is nothing short of business suicide.

5. **Your unique selling proposition**

The importance of focusing on customer benefits and offering customers a unique selling proposition has already been emphasised. By so doing it is possible to offer benefits to customers other than reduced prices and thus, to build your business from higher margin sales.

Every effort should be made to reinforce this principle.

ITEMS FOR ACTION NOW

Chapter 9

KNOW YOUR PRODUCT COSTS

The points made in the preceding chapter underpin the importance of knowing your product costs as the basis for sound decision making. Although inflation compounds the difficulties of keeping product costings up to date, it is nevertheless vital that this be done.

In the absence of reliable information on your firm's product costs you can only guess at the gross profit margins being achieved on each product. And guessing can lead to expensive mistakes. For example, when pricing products, when deciding which products to emphasise and which to delete — and in a host of other decisions.

At a minimum it is vital to have reliable information on the direct costs of each product and to be familiar with the principles of contribution accounting.

Chapter 10

RAISE THE PRODUCTIVITY OF SALES STAFF

To succeed in selling you must want to help people.

The aim of this chapter is to examine a variety of ways in which sales (or gross income) can be increased by raising the productivity of your sales staff.

A brief explanation regarding the concept of 'productivity' should be helpful here. Productivity concerns the relationship between inputs and outputs. Using sales as an example, productivity increases if either:

1. The existing sales staff achieve an increase in the volume of sales (same input of resources but increased output); or

2. Sales volumes are maintained at present levels, but by fewer sales staff (same output achieved from a lower input of resources).

The material following has been structured with the firm employing a field sales force in mind. Nevertheless many of the ideas discussed here are equally applicable to the management of sales staff in other environments. For example, in a retail store or other behind-the-counter situations.

The ideas following have been assembled under these headings:

1. Management of time

2. Sales targets and motivation

3. Remuneration

4. Recruitment

5. Communications with sales staff

6. Product knowledge

7. Selling techniques

8. Alternative forms of selling

1. **Management of time**

   (a) In consultation with individual sales staff have you undertaken an analysis of the time each salesman spends on his various activities?

The purpose of this exercise is of course, to find ways to increase the time spent in face-to-face selling. However, it is customary to find that many salesmen devote the majority of their time to activities such as travelling, waiting on customers, attending to administrative matters and paper work at the office, making service calls and doing other 'busy' work.

You may be surprised to find that as little as 1 hour per day (or less?) is actually devoted to face-to-face selling.

Having undertaken an analysis of how a salesman spends his time the next obvious step is to urgently reduce his non-productive work to a minimum, so that the time devoted to face-to-face selling can be increased.

(b) Are sales staff allocating their time sensibly between customers in proportion to those customers' sales potential?

(c) Are sales staff talking to those individuals who actually make the buying decisions in each customer organisation?

(d) Do sales staff plan their sales calls efficiently to minimise travelling distances and other non-productive time and cost?

(e) If your firm urgently needs a lift in sales it may be appropriate to instruct salesmen to reduce their coverage of the market, concentrating on those key customers who have the largest sales potential.

(f) Most salesmen have a favourite group of small customers. These may comprise customers who once purchased a lot but don't now, or people who have recently started to buy and promise to become big customers at a later date. Whatever the reason, small volume customers can be an expensive use of a salesman's time.

Can you afford the cost of salesmen devoting time to these customers?

(g) Could long distance customers be serviced at considerably lower cost by telephone calls, rather than having salesmen spend valuable time and cost driving to these customers and back?

2. Sales targets and motivation

(a) Does each salesman have a target which has been set in consultation with him?

(b) Are salesmen aware of the sales performance achieved by other salesmen and the sales objective for the firm as a whole?

(c) Have you identified clearly the specific factors that make **each** salesman work well, bearing in mind that each individual tends to be motivated by a different combination of elements in his job?

(d) What steps do you take to motivate salesmen to achieve their individual targets and to ensure their enthusiasm is sustained on a daily basis?

(e) Do you offer praise when a salesman performs well and try to focus on his strengths rather than on his weaknesses when counselling?

3. Remuneration

(a) In general salesmen tend to fall into two categories:

(i) Those who are goal-oriented and therefore motivated by financial incentives to achieve outstanding results; and

(ii) Those who have no real aims and are content to coast along, turning in a mediocre performance.

Bearing in mind the critical role of the sales function in your business, can you afford to employ the latter group?

How many of them are you presently employing on your sales staff?

(b) If you want to attract self-motivated, goal-oriented salesmen capable of producing outstanding results, what level of remuneration will you need to offer?

To what extent does your present remuneration scale fall short of this?

(c) Is your remuneration system geared to results so that outstanding salesmen are rewarded accordingly?

(d) Is your remuneration system structured to provide additional incentives for sales staff to concentrate on higher margin products?

4. Recruitment

(a) Before selecting sales staff do you identify those critical attributes which an appointee must have — knowing that if any are missing you are probably buying trouble?

(b) Do you offer remuneration which is high enough to attract outstanding new recruits to your sales force?

(c) What steps do you take to seek out and attract outstanding salesmen from other firms?

5. Communications with sales staff

(a) Do sales staff know the margins for each product and are they conscious of the need to concentrate on higher margin business?

(b) Do you deliberately try to seek out and remove frustrations sales staff may feel over matters such as inadequate stocks, too much paper work, slow response times for queries lodged with head office and so on?

(c) Do you talk to individual salesmen to get their personal views on matters such as:

(i) Ways of improving service to customers?

(ii) Competitors' strategies?

(iii) Other trends in the market, so your firm can formulate appropriate responses?

6. Product knowledge

(a) Does each of your sales staff have thorough knowledge of each product he is selling — remembering the impact which product knowledge (or lack of it) has on customers?

(b) How knowledgeable are your sales staff regarding competitors' products?

7. Selling techniques

(a) Apart from other attributes, do you deliberately seek to recruit sales staff who are pleasant, courteous and helpful in handling customers?

(b) Are your sales people thoroughly trained in sound selling techniques from the point of greeting a customer through to closing the sale?

In this context the following points are worthy of careful note:

(a) As a general rule it costs considerably more to cultivate a new customer than it does to sell repeat business to an existing satisfied customer.

(b) Dissatisfied customers will act as your 'public relations' people just as much as the satisfied ones.

(c) A key front line sales person in your firm will undoubtedly be your telephonist. Does she always handle customers and other callers courteously and efficiently? Have you tried phoning in to your own switchboard to find out?

8. Alternative forms of selling

The cost of maintaining a field sales force is rising continuously. Have you investigated alternative ways of generating sales such as telephone selling, direct mail or mail order?

These techniques could be used as possible supplements to, or in place of your existing selling methods. It could well be profitable to examine closely the pros and cons of alternative selling techniques.

Facts or opinion?

A range of key questions relating to raising the productivity of your sales staff have been put forward in this chapter. When reappraising each point ask yourself:

* How do I know this?

* Am I basing my answer to this question on facts or opinion?

ITEMS FOR ACTION NOW

Chapter 11

PURSUE FURTHER OPPORTUNITIES FOR GROWTH

The first job of a business manager is to convert social needs into profitable opportunities.

— Peter Drucker

Included here is a selection of further ideas for assisting sales and profit growth in your business. These are examined under the following headings:

1. Identify and exploit growth segments within your industry.

2. Different product versions for different market segments.

3. Guidelines for achieving flexibility.

1. Identify and exploit growth segments within your industry

Perhaps the best way to avoid some of the unpleasant realities of operating in a stagnant or shrinking industry is to concentrate on growth segments. Admittedly there are some industries for which it is virtually impossible to identify growth segments, but in most industries growth opportunities do exist.

For example:

(a) If your firm sells items of capital equipment for which orders are slumping, a likely growth strategy would be to pursue servicing and maintenance work. There is likely to be an increasing demand for servicing and maintenance business as customers will be concerned to ensure their existing equipment lasts longer.

(b) If your firm sells supplies to the building and construction industry and traditional sales are falling, a likely growth segment would be the home-handyman market. Particularly is this so since existing home owners will be concerned to save expense by carrying out alterations and repair work to their homes themselves. Moreover, home owners will probably tend to add on to their existing homes rather than upgrade to new homes as frequently as in the past.

(c) If your firm operates in the travel industry a likely growth segment in this market could be the older age groups — say 60 years plus.

Since the identification of growth segments usually requires a measure of insight and creativity, it is not possible to prescribe a standard set of procedures that will lead to their identification. Neverthless there is probably a way to think about most industries that should help identify growth segments. A key factor is to recognise that on close examination most industries comprise numerous segments and sub-segments. These can be defined along a variety of dimensions that should aid the identification of growth areas. For example: customer groups, price, product characteristics, product use, geographical areas and so on.

Collecting and analysing ideas from your staff could be particularly helpful here, as they may have some valuable input to contribute based on their own individual observations and experience.

Travelling to other countries to observe recent developments there may also be helpful in fuelling your ideas on growth opportunities within your industry.

Similarly studying relevant overseas trade journals could alert you to growth opportunities for your firm, based on emerging trends in overseas markets.

2. Different product versions for different market segments

Further growth potential could arise from marketing different versions of your products to cater specifically for different segments of the market.

For example, a higher quality, higher priced version of a particular product for those customers who want this and a lower quality, lower priced version for customers at the opposite end of the market.

3. Guidelines for achieving flexibility

In addition to coping with stagnant or declining markets and rising inflation, many businesses operate today in markets made still more volatile by a host of other factors. Rapid change and uncertainty about the future are predominant themes in today's volatile business environment.

Against this background building flexibility into your business to respond quickly to market changes is an important consideration, as you search for further growth opportunities.

Some broad guidelines to consider when assessing your firm's capacity to respond rapidly to market changes are:

(a) **Fixed assets**

The lower your firm's investment in fixed assets the greater the chances are that you can respond more quickly to change. For example:

(i) Specialised plant and equipment can become outmoded if demand patterns alter in the marketplace for the product(s) produced by this equipment. At that point it may be impossible to resell these assets.

(ii) Manufacturing firms tend to have a higher proportion of fixed costs than service-based businesses. As a general rule service businesses have greater flexibility to respond to market changes than manufacturing firms.

(b) **Leasing assets**

Leasing rather than purchasing assets offers the potential for maintaining greater cash flexibility. A detailed treatment of key considerations in the leasing of plant, equipment, motor vehicles and other assets is beyond our scope here. A firm contemplating leasing would be wise to seek competent, independent advice on all the various angles of this subject including taxation considerations.

(c) **Cash sales**

Selling for cash wherever possible rather than on credit eliminates the problems associated with debtors and again, assists cash flexibility.

(d) Selling to the end consumer

Engaging in a business operation in which you are selling to the end consumer of your product rather than to a 'middleman' means you are in direct contact with the end market. This offers three potential advantages:

(i) Your firm has direct control over the marketing of your products to the end user.

(ii) You are able to closely monitor consumer behaviour and market changes generally, at first hand.

(iii) Your firm gains more profit margin from each sale.

ITEMS FOR ACTION NOW

Chapter 12

DELETING PRODUCTS CAN RAISE PROFIT

Reinforce success. Abandon failure.

A professional gardener knows that on occasions he must prune his trees, shrubs and plants to keep them alive and healthy. So it is with a firm's products. From time to time products require pruning if they no longer make a profitable contribution to the well-being of the firm.

The need to consider product deletion decisions arises not only from changes in technology, but also from factors such as declining markets and rising inflation.

The case was cited earlier of the firm which has recently acquired considerable low margin business and now faces a critical shortage of cash. It was suggested that to ensure the firm's survival it may be necessary to severely cut back on low margin business to the point where the firm is operating from a smaller, profitable core of higher margin sales.

Retrenchment, negative growth, contraction in size, product deletion. In a volatile business environment these will continue to be critical elements in the survival and profit improvement programme of a business.

Management time and energy

A point frequently overlooked in this context is that weak products consume a disproportionate amount of management time and energy. Here we have a further example of the 80/20 principle already illustrated in earlier chapters.

If 80% of the effective results of a business are earned from only 20% of management's time, it is clear that most of management's work is relatively unproductive because it is devoted to the 'problems' of the business. By their very nature these problems are often the small volume, low margin, troublesome products and markets.

Questions to consider

Before making a final decision to delete a product or product line questions such as the following should be examined:

1. Is it possible to modify the product in any way to improve margins?

2. By how much can the price be increased dramatically or the product quality degraded — or both — either before abandonment or in place of it?

3. How much management time and resources can be freed up by deleting the product?

4. How much is the inclusion of this product in your firm's portfolio contributing to the sale of other products?

With regard to the last point, a frequent reason advanced by sales staff in support of retaining a weak product is that customers expect a complete product range and they will switch their business to competitors if the suspect product is abandoned. In many cases this argument does not hold true.

Compare alternative projections

There is one final test to be applied as the ultimate criteria upon which a product deletion decision should be based. This is to prepare and compare alternative projections of sales, costs and net profit showing:

1. The projected operating results of your firm with the suspect product(s) included; and

2. The projected operating results with the suspect product(s) deleted, after allowing for anticipated reductions in sales, direct costs and indirect costs.

A product deletion decision made without this form of analysis may amount to little more than guesswork.

Become a sales agency?

As a further thought, if your firm is engaged in manufacturing a product which is a candidate for deletion, could you discontinue manufacture and instead buy that product for resale from a former competitor or overseas supplier? This would maintain your present product offering intact and may be considerably more profitable.

ITEMS FOR ACTION NOW

Chapter 13

PRICING FOR PROFIT

In Chapter 1 the disastrous results which usually arise from reducing selling prices in a competitive/high inflation situation were illustrated. Yet the fact remains that many firms today are trying to buy back sales volumes in stagnant or declining markets by discounting prices 'because they must meet the competition'. Inflation and competition are controlling a firm caught in this predicament.

The rule to follow here is: Never reduce prices as a crisis measure when profits are low and the market is turning down. Competitors will follow suit. A price war will result or accelerate to the further detriment of your firm.

In Chapter 2 the advantages of raising selling prices as a route to profit growth were outlined. The point was also made that a relatively small increase in prices can have a dramatic effect in lifting net profit.

However, the usual objection to raising prices is that volume will decline as customers seek alternative suppliers. The central question then, is how your firm can raise selling prices without suffering a drop in the volume of business. Consider the following ideas as solutions to this question:

1. **Offer a unique selling proposition**

   Win the patronage of customers by focusing on a unique selling proposition as recommended in Chapter 6. Offer customers a unique benefit(s) which influences their decision to purchase from your business.

   Conversely to allow price to become the customer's dominant buying criteria is disastrous in a competitive/high inflation environment.

2. **Customer savings**

   Show the customer how he can reduce his purchasing costs. Many customers manage their purchasing function poorly. For example, they may order too frequently, order the wrong product for their requirements or require rush deliveries. Demonstrating to a customer how he can make savings by altering his buying pattern could more than offset the effect of your price increase to him.

3. **Small increases**

   It may be advantageous to raise prices in smaller increments rather than by large amounts. Large price rises may invite further competition.

4. Compare prices

Regularly compare your prices with those of competitors. Missing out on a 1% increase in price could have a considerable detrimental impact on your net profit, as illustrated in Chapter 2.

5. Compare terms of sale

Regularly compare your terms of sale with those of your competitors to see whether you are unnecessarily giving away some of your profit by way of freight, discounts or any other form of price reduction.

6. Discounts

Change the discount structure as a form of raising prices. Consider the possibility of variable discounts negotiated separately with each customer. If possible each discount arrangement should be specific over a particular period of time or over a specific delivery or order. This allows your firm the opportunity to renegotiate later.

7. Special services

Charge for special services rendered to customers.

8. Escalation clauses

Build price escalation clauses into contracts.

9. Small sellers and uneconomic products

Raise the prices of small selling lines and uneconomic products.

10. Price leading

Be a price leader. When you raise your prices the chances are competitors may well follow suit. This point may have particular application where your firm has a large share of the market.

11. Advance notice

Provide advance notice of the price increase to customers, allowing them the opportunity to stock up at old prices.

12. Lower price version

Introduce a new lower price, lower quality version of the product.

13. Alternative terms

Offer customers the option of alternative payment or service terms.

14. Seasonal rises

Raise prices on a seasonal basis where this is relevant.

15. Product presentation

Improve the packaging and/or presentation of the product and raise the price.

16. New product feature

'Trade up' by adding a new feature to the product and increase the price.

17. Slack purchasing procedures

Although most customers will want to negotiate the best terms they can get, it is a fact that some customers have slack purchasing routines and do not make comparisons between suppliers. It would be foolish not to take advantage of sloppy buying procedures where these exist in a customer organisation, provided this does not threaten your sales volume.

18. Justify price increases

Handle communications with customers regarding price increases in a professional manner. This should be an ongoing part of the work of sales staff. Salesmen should present customers with a good case for the price increase, pointing out how your firm's costs have increased and demonstrating ways in which your firm has reduced costs to minimise the price increase.

The objective of this exercise is to minimise the risk of customers regarding the price increase as being unfair. Care should be taken however, to avoid irritating customers by prolonging or otherwise overdoing explanations for price increases.

In conclusion it is worth noting that deteriorating business conditions are likely to promote pricing strategy to its proper place in management's order of priorities: at the top.

ITEMS FOR ACTION NOW

Chapter 14

HOW TO ADVERTISE — AND GET RESULTS

*In all probability in the minds of their planners and creators, the majority of advertisements are **intended** to persuade customers to buy the product being advertised. In actual fact due partly to a lack of really significant product superiority, a very high percentage of 'persuasion' ads are not persuasive at all: they are merely dressed-up 'reminders'. No one except the advertiser himself (and sometimes not even he) can say with certainty what a particular ad was **intended** to do. But on the basis of observation and analysis of a large number of ads, it would appear that by far the greatest number of them **actually do no more than provide a reminder.***

— *Clarence E. Eldridge*

If your firm advertises in any form of media, measure your current practice against these simple criteria for effective advertising:

1. What is the primary objective?

The first step in creating an advertisement should be to decide its primary objective. An advertisement can do the following things:

(a) It can inform.

(b) It can persuade.

(c) It can remind.

Most advertisements do not have a single purpose such as to inform **or** persuade **or** remind. On the contrary, they are likely to be framed with two or three of these purposes in mind, but in varying degrees of importance.

For example, the announcement of a new product or product improvement is intended **primarily** to convey information. A secondary purpose may well be to persuade the prospect of the product's merits and thus induce him to buy. But the primary emphasis should be on the informational aspect of the advertisement.

As a further example, an advertisement designed **primarily** to persuade can also provide information and at the same time, serve as a reminder. But in this case the major emphasis should be directed at making the persuasion as persuasive as possible.

The guidelines following assume that the primary objective of your firm's present advertising effort is the more urgent one of persuading prospects to purchase your products.

2. Target group

Have you identified the specific target group or market segment at whom the advertisement is to be aimed? For example, teenagers or housewives.

3. The consumer want or need

What consumer want or need is the advertised product intended to satisfy? Have you clearly identified this?

4. Product feature and consumer benefit

What feature of the advertised product contributes to the satisfaction of that want or need — and is the relationship between the product feature and the consumer benefit clearly explained?

It is important not only to explain your unique selling proposition, but also how this benefits the consumer. The advertisement should appeal to the customer's self interest. After all, the yardstick he will inevitably apply to your advertised product is 'What's in it for me?'

5. A unique benefit

The advertisement should not scatter its efforts or diffuse its impact. Thus as a general rule it is preferable to focus on one particular benefit, being the selected unique benefit to the customer.

6. Credibility and sincerity

If the advertisement claims product superiority over your competition is the claim supported by credible, persuasive proof or evidence — or at least believable argument?

The advertisement must 'ring true' and convey the impression of credibility and sincerity. To be avoided at all cost are wild, exaggerated or unsubstantiated claims. People won't believe them.

7. The headline

Does the headline capture the immediate attention of the reader and encourage him to read on?

A large measure of an advertisement's success lies in its headline. Particularly is this so since prospects are probably only scanning your advertising to begin with. The chances are much greater that prospects will pause and read the body of the copy if your headline captures their immediate attention.

Incorporating the unique customer benefit you are offering into the headline can be used very successfully as an attention-catching ploy.

8. **'You' and 'your'**

Use of these words gives your advertisement a personal impact, again especially in the headline.

9. **Is it simple, clear and complete?**

The best advertising is that which most closely resembles a personal solicitation, made in clear and simple terms and as representative as possible of real life.

On the other hand there appears to be a growing trend for some advertising agents to lose sight of the need for simplicity, clarity and indeed, many of the basic guidelines listed above. These agents appear to believe that advertising is part and parcel of show business. In designing advertisements they 'monkey with theatrics' consuming a large portion of advertising time and space with seemingly irrelevant gimmicks which have little in common with the basic principles listed here. This trend is most evident in television advertising.

To quote an American authority on advertising:

'We are now engaging in making a great deal of advertising a joke. And the question I think we must ask ourselves is: Whom are we kidding?'

To the foregoing principles then, should be added the need for simplicity, clarity and completeness. Furthermore, the language used should be simple and meaningful to prospective customers. There must also be no possibility of ambiguity.

10. Choice of media

Decide your advertising strategy first — then select the appropriate advertising media afterwards. Newspapers, radio, television and other media all have their particular strengths and disadvantages. For example, avoid the trap of deciding first to advertise on television before deciding on your advertising strategy. Using television may be a very expensive mistake if it fails to reach your target group or market segment — or fails to communicate your message with the right impact.

11. Does the advertisement make the sale?

If the objective of the advertisement is to persuade, it should establish a strong wish to buy on the part of prospective customers. You should be able to tell quickly that your sales have increased. If sales do not increase your problem could be one of the following:

(a) The advertisement has served merely as a dressed-up 'reminder' due to inadequate attention to a point(s) included in this chapter; or

(b) There could be one or more deficiencies in your firm's marketing process which **no** advertising can compensate for. For example: the advertised product is not readily available to customers at the point of sale; the unique customer benefit claimed in the advertisement does not exist in reality; or the advertised product is obsolete.

It is important to understand clearly that advertising has a communication function to perform. As such it cannot compensate for weaknesses associated with your products, selling procedures, distribution methods or other aspects of your marketing processes.

12. Changing your advertisements

It is not necessarily good practice to change your advertising frequently. Many firms do. But it should be remembered that some of the most successful advertisements (the ones that make the sales) are those that are retained intact and used repetitively over a considerable period of time.

Your customers are subjected to a continual barrage of advertising every day from many sources. If you want your advertising to perform its communication function effectively and thus assist in raising sales, it is important that your advertisements 'stand out'. Careful implementation of the principles listed above should ensure your advertising does just that.

ITEMS FOR ACTION NOW

Part C

REDUCING COSTS

Chapter 15

KEY ASPECTS OF COST REDUCTION

In those countries where inflation is a topic of concern we can confidently anticipate it will be so for many years to come, bringing continuous disturbance in its wake. Part of the problem is that the so-called 'solutions' invoked by politicians to 'cure the inflation problem' frequently have quite the reverse effect. In short, they increase inflation rather than reduce it.

Hence the critical importance of cost reduction as one of the three major routes to profit growth. What is required in a business is a continuous, committed effort on the part of all employees to operate a business more tightly. Every effort should be made to use resources more effectively and efficiently; to achieve more with less.

In this chapter key points relating generally to the subject of cost reduction are discussed. Subsequent chapters detail cost reduction measures applicable to specific cost areas within your business.

1. Cost reduction versus increasing sales

As a general rule, in most businesses cost reduction is a faster method of raising profit than driving for increased sales volume — at least in the short term. This is because:

(a) Increased sales volume requires time and effort to achieve in the more competitive marketing situations we are assuming here.

(b) Additional costs will inevitably be incurred in supporting increases in sales volume.

(c) On the other hand, once implemented the effect of a cost reduction measure on net profit is immediate.

(d) Each pound of cost saved represents a further extra pound of net profit before taxation for your business.

2. Competitors' response

Cost reduction measures do not usually invoke a response from competitors. By comparison, most other profit improvement measures (falling within the framework of increasing sales volumes or raising selling prices) are likely to require some consideration as to how competitors will respond.

3. Getting employee commitment

In practice the most difficult aspect of cost reduction is getting and maintaining commitment from employees. This frequently involves changing deeply entrenched attitudes of managers and staff who have hitherto given scant attention to economising on the firm's resources.

Outright hostility to cost saving measures is not uncommon. It must be made clear to employees that cost reduction is not some new form of autocracy, but rather a vital part of the process of business survival and hence, their continued employment.

4. Top management's example

Setting a personal example and maintaining a commitment to cost reduction at top management level is therefore of the utmost importance. The chief executive and senior managers must work hard at both the appearance and actuality of frugality. They should also create conditions in which both the temptation and opportunity to do things the expensive way are reduced or removed altogether.

5. Productivity improvements

A reduction in cost can be achieved not only by the traditional method of lowering total expenditure on a particular cost item, but also by achieving improvements in productivity. As explained earlier, productivity concerns the relationship between inputs and outputs. Productivity increases if either:

(a) The same quantity of resources (or inputs) are used to produce more outputs; or

(b) The same output is obtained from a lesser quantity of resources (or inputs).

For example, an improvement in the productivity of factory workers lowers the direct labour cost per unit of output and is thus a form of cost reduction. Similarly productivity improvements in respect of other cost items also result in cost reduction.

6. **Checklist of questions**

The following questions should be asked when examining any function, activity or expense item in your business:

(a) Can it be eliminated either in whole or in part, without significant harm to the firm's results?

(b) Does it do more than is required and can it therefore be reduced in scope and cost?

(c) On a management judgement basis, does it cost more than it is worth? In other words, do the costs exceed the benefits obtained?

(d) Can it be done more cheaply another way; for example, by using alternative procedures, equipment or people?

(e) If you were starting the business again from scratch would you include it?

(f) Can it be done more cheaply by an alternative service purchased from outside the firm?

(g) Can it be combined with some other activity or function?

(h) Can it be done less frequently?

(i) Is there any evidence of overlap or duplication of effort which should be eliminated?

(j) Are there any aspects of the activity or function which are not being done, but which should be added?

7. **Scrutinise all costs**

Never assume that any cost item is necessary. Take nothing for granted. Until a cost item is shown to be producing worthwhile results it should be suspect and subject to close scrutiny. In particular examine long standing practices, habits and routines within your business.

8. Examine large cost items first

Following the 80/20 principle it is probable that a small number of cost items will account for the bulk of your total expenses. For example, purchases and salaries and wages together may account for approximately 80% of your total costs. Or if yours is a service business, salaries and wages alone may comprise a substantial portion of your total expenses.

This suggests that to achieve maximum results quickly in cost reduction you should focus your attention first on these larger cost items. In the case of staff remuneration costs your primary concern should be to improve productivity by better utilisation of present staff.

9. Spending controls

Some businesses are inconsistent with their control on spending. For example, a decision to spend £10,000 on new plant may be the subject of an intensive investigation and a decision by top management. On the other hand, a decision to spend the same sum of money on raw materials might be left to a junior clerk.

It pays to review your spending controls to ensure that the benefit achieved in one area is not being undone in another.

10. Ask and train staff

It is a useful idea to seek the views of staff on ways and means of reducing costs in the particular area in which they work. They will often have useful input to contribute based on their own day-to-day observations and experience on the job.

Moreover, it pays to deliberately train staff to look for ways to cut costs so they are continually on the lookout for money-saving ideas.

11. Cost reduction teams

The subject of cost reduction is so important that larger firms may consider setting up a small, competent team of internal consultants to systematically review all corporate functions, searching for cost reduction measures.

This team may be given various names such as 'Profit Improvement Team' or 'Cost Improvement Unit'. One advantage of this move is that it demonstrates top management's determination that cost savings will be achieved.

The points listed in this chapter should be borne in mind when considering individual cost areas dealt with in the chapters following. To cite one example among many: the checklist of questions under item 6 could be usefully applied to a number of cost areas in most firms.

ITEMS FOR ACTION NOW

Chapter 16

MANAGE YOUR TIME FOR PROFIT

Tomorrow, you promise yourself, will be different.
Yet tomorrow is too often a repetition of today.

Managing your time as effectively as possible is important for three reasons:

1. Time is an expensive resource. For example, a salary of £20,000 per annum equates 20 pence per minute. And unlike most other resources, time is totally expendable. Time lost can never be retrieved.

2. You will need to make extra time available if you wish to give priority to implementing those ideas for profit improvement selected from this book.

3. Techniques you develop for using your own time more effectively can be passed on to other managers and staff, thereby resulting in further savings for your firm.

Listed below are some key points to help you manage your time more profitably.

1. **Analyse your time — and take corrective action**

   To save time you must first know where you are losing it. A simple method of accomplishing this is to keep a daily log — preferably for two or three days at least — in which you record how you use your time.

   Every quarter hour write in the log what you did for that period. Include a note of all interruptions, whatever their duration. At the end of each day add up the total time spent on each activity.

   Analysing how you spend your time in this way will probably disclose some surprising results — even shocks. For example:

   (a) Top priority tasks you know you should be doing may not be accomplished because you keep postponing them due to 'interruptions and unforeseen circumstances'.

   (b) Possibly the longest time you had without an interruption was 10-12 minutes.

(c) You will probably be disappointed at the amount of time you are spending on planning.

(d) A good portion of your work may be repetitive and could be delegated to subordinates.

(e) Certain employees take up a disproportionate amount of your time on trivial matters.

(f) You probably spend at least an hour a day on the telephone.

(g) Meetings may take up more time than they should because they 'drag on'.

Having identified the problem areas in the way your time is being consumed, you can then take appropriate action to eliminate them.

2. Priority list system

The simplest and most profitable way to plan the use of your time is to spend the last few minutes of each day writing out a list of top priority tasks for the following day. Ensure that the tasks on your list really are those top priority items you know you should be devoting your attention to. Then number these tasks in order of importance.

Start the next day with the most important task. Keep at it until it is completed and don't be concerned if you only finish the two or three most important tasks on your list — or even if you finish only one. The critical point is that you will be working on the most important tasks. The others can wait.

If you can't complete your top priority tasks using this system, you won't with any other method either. Moreover, without this simple system the chances are you may not even decide which are the top priority matters you should be giving your attention.

Once this system works for you, have your subordinates try it.

97

3. Delegation

In many businesses today managers are running out of time, yet their subordinates sometimes feel they are running out of work. Part of the problem here is usually due to a reluctance on the part of a manager to delegate because he feels that 'I can do it better myself'.

But delegation is critical if people are to gain experience and a firm is to grow and prosper. Some key points regarding delegation are:

(a) When delegating a task be sure to delegate **both** responsibility and authority.

Responsibility refers to the task to be done and decisions to be made, for which the subordinate must account.

Authority means the power necessary to enable the subordinate to fulfil his responsibility.

(b) Tasks and decisions should be delegated to the most junior person who has the necessary facts and capability to fulfil them. This saves considerable time for superiors.

(c) Even when you want to make a final decision yourself, it can save considerable time if you delegate the detailed work to others. Have them investigate the situation and refer back to you with several alternatives, with one alternative recommended.

4. Handle paper once

Handle each piece of paper only once. Many people spend their time organising and reorganising stacks of paper. Instead, divide papers into A, B and C piles. Place the A pile in a convenient drawer and the C pile in a not-so-convenient drawer. Take action on the A pile first, then the B's. The C items should be accumulated until you are either forced to do something about them or they are forgotten — in which case they should be thrown out.

5. Other time saving measures

There are numerous other ways in which you can help yourself to more time. The cumulative effect of these can be substantial. For example:

(a) Cut down on report writing. There is no substitute for eyeball-to-eyeball discussion.

(b) Use a dictating machine to answer correspondence. Alternatively let your secretary answer it herself. Or better still, write your reply on the original and mail it back.

(c) Hold fewer meetings. Start them an hour before closing time or hold them standing up, you included.

Remember the point made earlier: the time problems you are experiencing probably apply also to other managers and staff in your business. So after you have used the ideas listed in this chapter to help you manage your time more profitably, pass these ideas on to others so the benefits for your firm are multiplied.

ITEMS FOR ACTION NOW

Chapter 17

RAISE PRODUCTIVITY THROUGH PEOPLE

Chapter 10 dealt specifically with the question of how to raise the productivity of sales staff. This particular chapter relates to all employees — managers and staff — across the various sections or functions of your business, whatever its size.

Although a firm does not 'own' its managers and staff, there can be no question that they are its most important resource. Thus in a declining market/high inflation environment it becomes imperative to ensure that the 'people' resource is being managed effectively and efficiently.

The ideas presented below for enhancing productivity are grouped under these heading:

1. Examine your organisation structure

2. Set high recruitment standards

3. Sound training enhances productivity

4. Measure performance by results

5. Job enrichment

6. Exit interviews

1. Examine your organisation structure

Scrutinise your firm's organisation structure carefully, looking for improvements in organisational design. For example:

(a) Is your firm organised on a geographic (or branch) basis where a divisional structure organised by major product groupings would be more appropriate?

(b) Is the 'span of control' appropriate in each case? The span of control (synonyms are: span of management, span of supervision, span of responsibility) refers to the number of subordinates under the control of a given supervisor or manager.

The span of control question is important because a wrong choice of span can harm the efficiency of a firm. With too few supervisors productivity declines; with too many, supervisory costs are unnecessarily high. There is no set formula for determining how many staff should report to each supervisor or manager. Each case needs to be examined individually.

(c) Is there any evidence of vague reporting relationships? This means that staff are unclear as to whom they report — and who reports to them. For example, it is not uncommon to find one man reporting to two superiors.

(d) Have you sought the ideas of staff on how procedures such as work flow could be improved?

Organisational weaknesses in key areas such as those cited above affect productivity so profoundly that it is doubtful whether a successful profit improvement programme can be carried out in the absence of a sound organisation structure.

2. Set high recruitment standards

A declining market/high inflation business environment demands considerably more creativity and stamina from managers and staff than a buoyant business situation. Therefore as a general principle it is wise when recruiting new employees to 'go after the best talent you can find' for each particular job to be filled. To reiterate: your people resource is your most important resource.

The following points also relate to recruiting and selecting new managers and staff:

(a) The first step in this process is to clearly define the key requirements of the job position to be filled, as a benchmark against which the attributes of each applicant can then be assessed.

(b) A level of remuneration should be offered which is **fully** commensurate with the requirements of each job position, in order that good quality applicants are attracted to apply.

(c) Consider using part-time staff where this is appropriate. Actual experience by businessmen points to the fact that part-time staff are frequently very productive and reliable. Particularly is this true of married women whose children are at or beyond school age, and who are keen to obtain part-time employment. There is a rich labour pool here well worth tapping.

3. Sound training enhances productivity

Consider:

(a) Does each member of your staff have the necessary knowledge and skills to carry our his/her job efficiently?

(b) How do you know this?

It is well worth spending time and money training new employees and retraining existing staff where necessary. This will inevitably save you far more in increased productivity than it costs.

To be effective training must be supported by a positive commitment on the part of senior management. Without this support training will become an ad hoc exercise. The net result of this will inevitably be a deterioration in product quality, service to customers — and profitability.

4. Measure performance by results

When assessing the performance of a firm attention is focused on the firm's results, usually expressed as some measure of profitability. Likewise in assessing the performance of an employee attention should be focused on the **outputs** or results of his work and the extent to which these contribute to the firm's profit objective.

This implies the need for a job description or 'Key Results Specification' for each person in your firm, whereby agreement is reached with each employee concerning:

(a) A defined and agreed parcel of work for which he is responsible; and

(b) The end results (or outputs) for which he is accountable.[1]

A simple but practical format for a Key Results Specification is shown in Figure 6.

FIGURE 6

Key Results Specification		
POSITION:		
My key tasks are:	My authority is:	I am effective if I achieve these key results:

Particular points to note regarding Figure 6 are:

(a) Limits of authority are defined in the second column.

(b) The final column identifies the performance standards agreed with the individual for each key task. These standards (or key results) should be quantified so that actual results achieved can subsequently be measured against the agreed standards.

If any manager or staff member is to be held accountable for results, three conditions must exist:

(a) He must know and agree with what is expected of him — his key results.

(b) He must have the authority and the necessary resources to enable him to achieve his key results.

(c) He must know what his results are — his actual performance.

If any of these three conditions is missing he cannot be held accountable.

5. **Job enrichment**

Out of the many investigations in various countries into the subject of human motivation in work situations one theme has emerged continually: the concept of job enrichment.

These studies demonstrate that the work situations people find most satisfying are generally those in which the following conditions exist:

(a) The work is challenging.

(b) The employee has a clear understanding of his objectives.

(c) **Praise and appreciation are expressed by a superior when an employee does a good job. His efforts are recognised.**

(d) There is scope for additional responsibility and personal advancement.

These factors lead to enthusiasm, satisfaction and increased productivity.

To what extent are these factors present — or absent — in your firm?

For example, consider item (c) regarding praise and recognition. To what extent do you estimate that productivity and hence, profits could be increased in your business if the principle in item (c) alone was practised consistently?

On the other hand, the work situations people find most dissatifying are usually characterised by the following:

(a) Staff are not kept well informed of changes affecting them within the firm.

(b) Supervision of work is poor and staff are side-tracked from their major tasks.

(c) Pay and working conditions are felt to be inadequate.

(d) Staff are given conflicting instructions from different sources.

(e) Praise is rarely given when an employee does a good job.

These latter factors cause frustration and lowered productivity. They should obviously be watched for and remedied as quickly as possible.

Again, to what extent are these factors present in your firm?

6. Exit interviews

A simple but informative way of learning more about the strengths and weaknesses of your business is to interview employees who resign. Frank discussion with them should help you to pinpoint areas of weakness which are causing frustration and thus, lowered productivity.

To obtain maximum benefit from an 'exit interview' it is important to prepare a list of frank questions to enable you to probe thoroughly into the real reasons why the employee being interviewed is resigning. Based on this information appropriate action can then be taken to remedy weaknesses, thus raising productivity.

ITEMS FOR ACTION NOW

Chapter 18

ACHIEVE PEAK EFFICIENCY IN PURCHASING AND STOCK CONTROL

For a firm marketing physical products, purchases of incoming materials or goods for resale typically comprise a substantial cost item. Because of the importance of the purchasing function it offers considerable potential for cost savings. This is particularly so since it is usual for top management to devote considerably more attention to sales than to the purchasing function.

In the short term at least and possibly on a continuing basis, your firm may be able to achieve greater profit improvements from raising purchasing efficiency than from boosting sales volumes.

Thus the impact on net profit of a reduction in the cost of purchases can be dramatic. This point is illustrated in Figure 7 where a 5% reduction raises net profit by 35%.

FIGURE 7

ABC Company Ltd (a non-manufacturing concern)

Illustration of the effect on net profit of a 5% reduction in the cost of purchases

	Before £	After 5% reduction £
SALES	500,000	500,000
Less purchases	350,000	332,500
Gross trading profit	150,000	167,500
Less other operating costs	100,000	100,000
NET PROFIT BEFORE TAXATION	£50,000	£67,500
% increase in net profit		+35%

Similarly if your firm is a manufacturing concern the same principle applies regarding the potential impact on net profit of cost savings in raw materials and incoming supplies.

Calculating relevant figures for your firm will give an appreciation of the importance in net profit terms of achieving peak efficiency in the purchasing function.

Turning to the question of stock control: If your firm's stock levels are higher than they need be to support your sales, the result is excess money tied up in stocks. If you can lower your stock levels without damaging sales you can release cash for use elsewhere in the business.

The cost of holding stock is considerable and typically between 15% and 35% of total indirect costs. This may not be apparent since these costs are 'hidden' within a variety of cost areas such as:

* Interest on funds tied up in stock

* Insurance

* Rent and other costs of storage facilities

* Damage to stock

* Stock obsolescence

* Shrinkage

* Cost of handling stock

* Cost of keeping stock records

So again, achieving peak efficiency in stock control can enhance profit considerably.

Techniques for improving efficiency in purchasing and stock control are listed below under these headings:

1. Purchasing procedures

2. Improvements in product design

3. Goods inwards and payment procedures

4. Stock control

1. Purchasing procedures

(a) Is your purchasing officer aware of the financial ramifications of cost reductions he achieves — that is, their effect in raising net profit?

(b) Is your purchasing officer continually on the lookout for alternative suppliers who can give you the same products at a lower cost?

There is often a tendency to become 'locked in' to the same suppliers, thus losing the benefit of lower prices available elsewhere.

(c) Offering prompt payment to suppliers in exchange for a discount could be worth considering.

(d) Guaranteeing continuity of orders to a particular supplier in exchange for a larger discount could be profitable.

(e) Have your purchases of some lines increased to the point where you qualify for volume discounts, but the supplier has not granted these to you?

(f) Potentially the largest savings can be made by giving special attention to those 20% of products which comprise 80% of the total value of your purchases.

(g) When buying extra quantities to obtain volume discounts calculate the extra costs involved in interest, storage and insurance charges to ascertain whether the discount is really worthwhile.

(h) Purchasing increased quantities of a product before an expected price rise is not always profitable. The purchase may cause cash flow problems, together with increased storage and other costs. There may also be a risk that demand for the product concerned could reduce.

(i) If you anticipate industrial unrest in a company which supplies your business it may pay to purchase more of that company's products to cover this eventuality.

(j) You may be able to lower your purchasing costs for some items by setting up a bulk buying arrangement in conjunction with a competitor(s) in your area.

(k) Is your purchasing officer constantly on the lookout for alternatives to the products you presently buy?

(l) Survey your existing suppliers asking them if there are any ways in which you can lower the unit cost of your purchases. For example, your enquiries may reveal that your firm is ordering in uneconomic batches or insisting on something minor which adds considerably to the price of a product(s).

If your firm can help a supplier save money you should both be able to negotiate a reduction in cost without damaging the supplier's net profit.

(m) Be courteous to your suppliers' sales people. It costs nothing and if you do, the chances are they will try harder to negotiate better terms for you.

(n) Try to secure longer credit terms from a new supplier at an early stage when he is anxious to do business.

(o) Maintaining good communications between the purchasing function and other departments can play an important part in cost reduction. For example, involving the purchasing officer in decisions to eliminate any of your firm's products can avoid over-stocking of unwanted materials.

(p) Buying from two competing suppliers can be beneficial. This way both suppliers will be keen to give you good service as they will both want a greater share of your business.

(q) Consider opportunities for purchasing merchandise on consignment, paying for it only after it is sold.

(r) Are there any components presently being made in-house which could be purchased more cheaply from an outside supplier?

(s) Conversely, can your firm make more cheaply any components presently being bought outside?

(t) Can you reduce wastage by ordering materials precut to correct lengths for your purposes?

2. Improvements in product design

(a) It could prove to be a useful cost saving measure to obtain samples of your competitors' products and have a physical examination made of these to determine differences in the materials, construction, and function of the competitors' products versus your own.

Examining products in this way can trigger useful cost reduction ideas and may even improve the functioning of your products.

(b) You may find your competitor has developed some new materials or a particular manufacturing technique to help reduce cost. Perhaps you can do likewise.

Alternatively he may have redesigned his product to better recognise the functional needs of the customer. This could make his product more attractive to use or result in lower costs — or both.

(c) Aside from examining competitors' products, consider these questions:

(i) Are you over-specifying the quality of materials required?

(ii) Are engineering tolerances too high and could these be reduced without impairing product quality to the customer?

3. Goods inwards and payment procedures

(a) Are all incoming materials and purchases carefully checked as to the quantity received and marked off clearly against the delivery docket?

(b) Similarly, is a quality check carried out on all incoming items? If an item is found to be faulty this is the point at which it should be identified and returned to the supplier.

(c) Is rigid security maintained over the inwards goods area and is it supervised by efficient and loyal staff?

(d) When paying for purchases the delivery docket should be carefully matched with the supplier's invoice and all quantities and calculations thoroughly checked.

It is often a lack of attention to the most fundamental points in operating a business which costs a firm dearly. The items listed above come within the scope of this principle.

4. **Stock control**

(a) As pointed out earlier the cost of holding stock is considerable. A primary focus in stock management should therefore be on reducing stock levels to a minimum consistent with meeting sales requirements.

(b) It is important to calculate your firm's stock turnover rate and to compare this with

(i) Past periods for your firm; and

(ii) Other firms in your industry, if this information is available.

The formula for this calculation is:

$$\frac{\text{Cost of sales}}{\text{Average of (opening stock + closing stock)}}$$

Improving your rate of stock turn reduces those costs listed earlier in this chapter (interest, insurance, rent and other costs of storage facilities, damage to stock and so on).

(c) If you are holding stock which is not selling it may be more profitable to quit it at reduced prices rather than have your funds tied up for a long period.

(d) Consider further ways of reducing pilferage if this is a problem. For example:

  (i) Use tighter security measures.

  (ii) Use alternative forms of transport for carrying products to and from your firm.

  (iii) Use floor walkers in a retail situation.

(e) A reduction in the number of stock holding points (or warehouses) may give a cost saving which more than offsets the cost of freighting items to outlying destinations.

(f) Are goods handled, stacked and stored with due care to avoid breakage and/or other damage?

(g) If you are a manufacturer, are production facilities well laid out to minimise material handling and ensure a balanced work flow?

(h) In manufacturing it may be more profitable to make longer production runs of low volume products. The costs of maintaining higher stocks may be more than offset by the reduced costs of setting up less often. Alternatively, if your set-up costs are low it may be more economical to make smaller production runs.

ITEMS FOR ACTION NOW

Chapter 19

ARE YOU MINIMISING TAXATION?

In a high inflation situation taxation imposes an ever increasing burden on a business. One of the key problems of course, is that a firm has to find cash to meet its taxation payments which are calculated on 'paper' profits and not real earned profits.

Minimising taxation thus becomes an issue of crucial importance. In this regard it is vital to seek and obtain the services of a competent taxation consultant or chartered accountant. Particularly is this so for the smaller business. However, larger firms can also benefit from calling in a competent tax adviser where the necessary expertise does not exist internally within the firm.

Taxation legislation is continually changing and becoming more complex. This further underlines the importance of obtaining the services of a competent tax adviser who is familiar with recent changes in the law and its application to business.

A thorough tax specialist will probe all areas of a business looking for tax saving measures which are available to your firm within the framework of current tax legislation and practice.

Are you sure your firm's taxation liability is being minimised to the full extent possible?

Is it possible that the cost of a few hours spent with a top-flight tax specialist may reveal ways to achieve meaningful tax savings for your firm?

ITEMS FOR ACTION NOW

Chapter 20

CRITICALLY EXAMINE YOUR INFORMATION SYSTEM

In volatile business conditions it is important

(a) That you have regular and reliable information regarding your firm's operating results.

(b) That operating results are compared against your profit and cash flow plans discussed in Chapters 4 and 5;

(c) As the basis for taking corrective action where necessary. This point is dealt with further in Chapter 25.

Your accounting and other information may be produced manually, by mechanical methods or by computer. Whatever the system used, examine it critically against these criteria:

1. **Chart of accounts**

    Is your information system based on a clearly defined chart of accounts with revenues and costs accumulated under precise headings relevant to your information needs?

2. **Reports**

    Are you receiving

    ★ clearly presented reports

    ★ in the formats **you** require

    ★ produced on time, and

    ★ measuring your actual progress?

    Producing a set of accounts each month may be an unnecessary cost. But actual operating results for key indicators such as sales and major expense items will enable you to monitor your progress on a monthly basis against your profit plan described in Chapter 4.

3. **Simplicity**

    Simplicity is a vital criteria against which any information system should be assessed. For example, complex or unnecessary reports which are of no value for decision making purposes are an unnecessary cost and should be eliminated.

4. Staff Training

Are each of your accounting (and data processing) staff well trained to carry our their particular jobs? If errors occur in the processing of transactions the inevitable result will be inaccurate reports.

5. Record keeping systems

Review record keeping systems in your office against questions such as these:

(a) Do you use all the data staff are compiling?

(b) Is there duplication in record keeping which should be eliminated?

(c) Are records kept as simple as possible, consistent with information requirements? For example, the preparation of numerous reconciliations may be an indication that the records being maintained are too complex.

ITEMS FOR ACTION NOW

Chapter 21

SPEED UP COLLECTIONS FROM DEBTORS

If your firm sells on credit terms it is important to collect debts owing by customers as promptly as possible for four reasons:

(a) Excess funds tied up in debtors reduces cash available for use elsewhere in the business.

(b) Your firm will inevitably be incurring interest charges on funds borrowed to finance the overdue accounts.

(c) The time and effort involved in chasing collections from debtors costs money.

(d) A bad debt is a straight financial deduction from your firm's net profit.

Techniques for speeding up collections from debtors and avoiding bad debts can be grouped into two broad categories:

(a) Steps to take up to the point of sale; and

(b) Credit collection procedures.

Each of these categories is now dealt with in turn.

Steps to take up to the point of sale

1. Obtain cash sales wherever possible. For example, train counter staff to sell for cash rather than making the offer to a customer: 'Do you wish to charge this to your account?'

2. Offering a discount for 'cash with order' sales may be appropriate in some cases.

3. Weed out slow paying accounts and in future sell to these on a 'cash in advance' or 'cash on delivery' basis.

4. An alternative procedure might be to set up a draft and draw on the customer for payment either in full or in part, before releasing your product. This could apply for example, if you are selling expensive items or if you doubt the financial strength of the customer.

5. Establishing an approved list of customers with a credit limit applicable in each case is a recognised procedure in many firms.

6. Where applicable, visit a prospective customer's place of business and look for any visible signs of inability to pay debts. Use your judgement as to whether this business gives the outward appearance of being a satisfactory credit risk.

7. The salesman must ensure that his firm's terms of sale are clearly defined in writing and brought to the customer's attention. These terms will normally cover items such as the terms of payment, terms of delivery to the customer, any warranties or guarantees and so on.

8. Questioning the customer as to the purpose for which he is buying your product will help to ensure he is buying the most appropriate product from your range to meet his particular needs.

9. Supplying a sample of the product to the customer so he can check the product is exactly what he wants, could also help.

10. Check to ensure the customer's purchase order complies fully with your own terms of sale.

11. Accomplish each sale courteously and thoroughly, giving the customer good service and a favourable impression of the way you do business. This should not only enhance the chances of repeat business, but also assist in obtaining prompt payment from the customer.

12. Ensure the details on your packing slip are complete and accurate. This is likely to be an important document in the customer's approval-for-payment procedures.

13. Send a copy of your invoice either with the product or promptly thereafter. Bill promptly for all goods and services. If you are providing a service to a client spread over a period of several months, arrange with the client that you will bill him on an interim basis as the work progresses.

Credit collection procedures

1. Invoices and monthly statements must be processed efficiently and quickly so these documents are received by customers in plenty of time to be included in their accounts payable procedures.

2. Some firms prefer to send second copies of their invoices stapled to their monthly statements, the first copy having been despatched at the time of sale.

3. Are your invoices and statements always clear, complete and accurate? If not there is a risk the customer will use any flaws in your documentation as an excuse for delaying payment.

4. If your firm adopts the common practice of including an aged analysis of the balance brought forward on customers' statements, this procedure may be to your disadvantage. This may well encourage the debtor to select and pay only part of the total amount owing. For example, the oldest portion of the debt.

   Several firms with whom the author has worked have discontinued the practice of aging the balances brought forward on customer statements. This move has assisted considerably in speeding up the collection of overdue balances from debtors.

5. Regardless of the procedures you use to follow up overdue accounts, prompt action is very important. As a general rule the longer a debt remains outstanding the harder it becomes to collect.

6. Use your aged trial balance as an action document. Write alongside each overdue amount the action to be taken and initiate this right away.

7. When following up overdue accounts try to distinguish between:

   (a) Those customers who are withholding payment due to a query or complaint. For example, the receipt of faulty goods.

   (b) Those customers who want to pay, but who have a temporary lack of funds.

(c) Those customers who want to pay, but are unlikely to have sufficient funds to pay in full.

(d) Those who have no intention of paying.

8. Ensure your sales staff have sufficient financial knowledge to understand the importance of cash collections from debtors and that 'a sale is not complete until the cash is in the bank'. It is sales staff, not the accounting staff, who should be involved where necessary to assist in collecting overdue accounts.

9. A telephone call by sales staff can often obtain payment more quickly than a letter and it is usually cheaper. Assume in the first place the account is being withheld for payment owing to a query or complaint by the customer. If this is the case, deal with these matters immediately and politely remind the customer of the agreed terms of payment.

10. If the customer's complaint involves a trivial matter and cannot be readily resolved, it is usually cheaper to issue him with a credit note at once rather than pursuing the matter further. Moreover, he may be withholding payment of the full amount due until his trivial complaint is resolved.

11. If the customer offers an excuse for withholding payment (and therefore probably has a lack of funds) the next step is to arrange a payment plan, with regular instalments to be paid by the customer over an agreed period. This may be arranged either over the telephone or by the salesman making a personal visit to a senior person in the customer's organisation.

If possible obtain from the debtor a series of post-dated cheques for the agreed progress payments and bank these as they fall due.

12. When pursuing a difficult overdue account it is usually sound policy to refer the matter directly to a senior person in the customer's organisation. For example, the chief financial executive or one of the cheque signatories.

A further useful move could be to bring the overdue account to the attention of a key person in the customer's organisation who relies upon your product. For example, the factory manager.

13. A further point in favour of using telephone calls or personal visits to recover outstanding debts (as opposed to writing to the debtor) is that both these are ready methods of identifying bad debt risks early on. Information gleaned about the customer including any evasive behaviour, can usually be detected during a telephone call or personal visit.

Furthermore, a telephone call or a personal visit is harder for the debtor to ignore than a mere letter urging him to pay.

14. If the overdue debtor is one of your continuing customers you could arrange to supply him with say,£50 worth of product for every £100 he pays you. You can then use the remaining £50 to gradually extinguish the overdue debt.

15. If you charge interest on overdue accounts be sure

(a) To include this in the terms of sale, and

(b) To enforce it.

16. It may be helpful in some circumstances to grant small discounts to clients who pay within the prescribed credit period.

17. Obviously employing a collection agency or solicitor to recover an overdue debt should be used only as a last resort. If a customer is willing but unable to pay, you will probably collect more in the long run by resorting to the methods listed above.

ITEMS FOR ACTION NOW

Chapter 22

PUT NON-PRODUCTIVE ASSETS TO WORK

In a declining market/high inflation environment it is vital that all your firm's assets are as productive as possible, thereby assisting to maximise profit and cash flow.

Particular points to note are as follows:

1. Cash management

Methods of improving efficiency in selected aspects of cash management have been dealt with in earlier chapters. Further matters to watch are:

(a) Eliminating unnecessary bank accounts assists tighter, centralised control over cash resources.

(b) Bank all receipts promptly. Never permit funds to lie idle.

2. Sale of investments

Examine your latest balance sheet and other records for any investments which might be sold, where these funds could earn higher rates of return in the principle activities of the business.

3. Sale of fixed assets

When a firm has a large proportion of its capital tied up in fixed assets it may be appropriate to release some of these funds for working capital purposes. This can be achieved in a number of ways. For example:

(a) Sell idle or under-utilised assets for cash.

(b) Enter into a sale and leaseback arrangement with a leasing company so your firm retains the use of those assets, but also receives an injection of cash.

(c) Sell off selected assets for cash and purchase the services those assets provided from outside vendors.

(d) If additional fixed assets are required consider

    (i) Leasing as an alternative to outright purchase; or

    (ii) Buying the assets on an extended payment plan.

4. Reassess special projects

It may also be prudent to reappraise any special projects your firm is contemplating or presently engaged upon. For example: capital commitments either intended or already entered into, research and development projects, computer systems projects and any other projects of a special nature.

A problem with these projects is that costs frequently become so much higher and revenues so much less than originally estimated that this causes unexpected drains on a firm's cash resources.

Of course this does not mean that all special projects should be abandoned. The point being made here is that they should be carefully reappraised

(a) To check that the original assumptions as to revenues, costs and time schedules are still valid; and

(b) To ensure your firm's assets are being deployed as productively as possible.

If a careful reappraisal of a particular project indicates that the project is now suspect, appropriate remedial action should be taken quickly. Circumstances may call for immediate modification or even deletion of the project.

ITEMS FOR ACTION NOW

Chapter 23

REDUCE OTHER COSTS

Chapters 15 to 22 have dealt with a variety of techniques for reducing those costs typically of major concern to most businesses. However, your business will also be incurring other expense items not treated specifically in earlier chapters. For example, motor vehicle expenses, insurance premiums, travelling expenses, telephone and tolls and so on.

The following points relate to reducing these further cost items:

1. Attention should be focused in the first instance on your largest cost items because this is where the maximum potential for cost savings is likely to be.

2. However, every effort should be made to achieve savings in **all** the various cost areas of your business.

3. The key points relating to cost reduction listed in Chapter 15 should prove to be helpful as you tackle each cost item.

To reiterate a point made earlier: Each pound of cost saved represents a further pound of net profit before tax for your business.

ITEMS FOR ACTION NOW

Part D

IMPLEMENTING CHANGES

Chapter 24

GET COMMITMENT TO PROFIT IMPROVEMENT

As a manager your primary task is to achieve your firm's profit objective or that portion of it for which you are accountable, through people. This means that if you are to be successful in implementing ideas from earlier chapters to lift your profit, you will need the commitment and cooperation of others in your firm.

This will need to be obtained at three levels:

1. Subordinates and staff in your section. (If you are the chief executive this means managers and staff throughout your firm).

2. Your superiors — where you are not the chief executive.

3. Board of directors.

Particular points relating to each of these three groups are set out below.

1. **Subordinates and staff in your section**

   Key matters relating to the question of getting the commitment and cooperation of the people in your section are:

   (a) People will respond favourably only to those changes they perceive to be relevant. The relevancy criteria means that staff will need adequate explanations as to **why** particular changes aimed at lifting net profit are needed. Otherwise they will resist changes they do not understand.

   (b) Giving explanations to subordinates and staff usually means imparting various degrees of financial knowledge and other facts about your firm, its objectives and its opportunities and problems.

   (c) It is important to seek the views of subordinates and staff as much as possible when implementing changes to improve profit. In this way people feel a greater sense of involvement.

   (d) You will probably be able to implement only a few major changes simultaneously — otherwise you run the risk of confusing your subordinates and staff. You will therefore need to establish your priorities for profit improvement changes.

It is a wise move to place at the top of your list not only fundamental changes carrying the potential for making the most impact on profit in the long run, but also a few dramatic and highly visible changes that can be made and seen to be successful very quickly.

(e) Figure 8 sets out a suggested format for a Profit Improvement Worksheet.

FIGURE 8

PROFIT IMPROVEMENT WORKSHEET

Objective of the the project:

Person responsible:

Date discussed:

Target date for completion:

Agreed action:

Resources needed:

Progress reviews:

| No.1 | No.2 |

Project completed:

Results achieved:

Matters arising — for further follow-up:

Signed ....

Date ....

The purposes of the worksheet in Figure 8 are:

(i) To serve as a record of points agreed between you and the person to whom you delegate responsibility and authority for implementing a particular change; and

(ii) To provide a means for following up on progress to date and the final results achieved.

Figure 8 can of course, be modified in any way you wish to suit your particular needs.

2. Your superiors

As with other business decisions, the wholehearted commitment and support of your superiors is needed to ensure success in implementing changes to raise profit.

When seeking their support it will be necessary to 'sell' them the benefits of your proposed changes. This means quantifying the estimated impact of these changes in dollar terms on sales, costs and net profit.

3. Board of directors

Likewise the board of directors must be involved in changes to lift profit. Indeed, they have an important role to play in initiating and implementing profit improvement projects.

Exercise continual, strong follow-up

Inevitably there will be problems in implementing improvements to raise profit. You will find it necessary to exercise continual, strong follow-up to ensure changes that have been initiated are carried through to obtain the desired results by the agreed target dates. The Profit Improvement Worksheet in Figure 8 should prove useful in this regard.

When something goes wrong in the course of implementing a change remember that the first rule is 'Don't panic'. Offer your subordinates and staff help to get them back on the course needed to achieve the desired results.

Reward results

Finally, good results achieved on the part of subordinates and staff in implementing profit improvement changes should be rewarded. Praise, promotion, financial payments and other appropriate rewards will help to motivate staff to further achievements in lifting profit.

ITEMS FOR ACTION NOW

Chapter 25

MONITOR PROGRESS AND TAKE CORRECTIVE ACTION

The great thing in the world is not so much where we stand, as in what direction we are moving.

— *Oliver Wendell Holmes*

Chapters 4 and 5 dealt with the importance of establishing a profit plan (or operating budget) and a cash flow plan for the current financial year. To ensure your profit plan and cash flow plan serve their purpose it is crucial that:

1. Actual progress is plotted regularly against your plans, and

2. Corrective action is taken promptly if actual results fall behind the plans.

As pointed out in Chapter 20, for purposes of comparing actual results against your profit plan it may be a time consuming and unnecessary expense to prepare a complete operating statement each month. Instead, comparing actual results for key indicators such as sales (or gross income) and larger expense items should enable you to track progress satisfactorily against your profit plan.

Manage by pulse beats — not post mortems

Promptness is of the essence when comparing results and taking corrective action. This means firstly, that actual results must be available quickly after the period to which they relate and secondly, that corrective action must be taken immediately where actual results for sales, expenses or cash flow are falling behind the plans.

In this way you manage your business by pulse beats — not post mortems.

Corrective action

Corrective action may take various forms depending upon the circumstances. When resolving a problem remember that as a general rule it is more important to solve 90% of the problem with a quick but somewhat imperfect solution, than to go after the last 10% but take three times as long to produce results.

Corrective action may include introducing further ideas for increasing sales volumes, raising prices or reducing costs — as contained in preceding chapters.

ITEMS FOR ACTION NOW

Chapter 26

PLAN LONGER TERM STRATEGY

We live in an era when rapid change breeds fear, and fear too often congeals us into a rigidity which we mistake for stability.

— Lynn White, Jr.

155

It was stated at the outset that:

> 'The objective of this publication is to present and explain practical, down-to-earth techniques you can use **now** to lift the profit of your business.'

Thus the emphasis throughout has been a 'here and now' one, focusing on immediate ways of improving your profit and cash flow in the short term.

This publication would be incomplete however, if it failed to draw attention to the importance of responding to external changes by planning longer term strategy for the 1980's. Although a detailed treatment of this important subject is beyond our scope here, there are a number of key points which should be mentioned briefly.

A systematic corporate planning procedure involves:

1. Establishing a firm's long term objectives.

2. Critically examining the firm to identify its major strengths and weaknesses.

3. Forecasting important changes and trends likely to occur in the future environment in which the firm will operate. These are classified as either 'opportunities' or 'threats'.

4. Determining a long term strategy to carry the firm forward in a manner which allows it to take advantage of opportunities and avoid threats.

Changes in the future environment examined in a systematic corporate planning system are usually grouped under these headings:

1. Political

2. Social

3. Economic

4. Technological

5. Competitive

In chapter 11 some guidelines were suggested for building flexibility into your business to assist in responding to external changes. These should also be considered within the context of longer term corporate strategy.

If the matters referred to in this chapter seem too sophisticated and remote to deserve attention, it should be remembered that we live in a decade of rapid change. A business which chooses to ignore at least the fundamental principles of longer term corporate planning may do so at its peril. Furthermore, such is the pace of change that longer term business strategies need to be reviewed continually.

ITEMS FOR ACTION NOW

ITEMS FOR ACTION NOW

ITEMS FOR ACTION NOW

ITEMS FOR ACTION NOW

ITEMS FOR ACTION NOW

ITEMS FOR ACTION NOW

ITEMS FOR ACTION NOW

ITEMS FOR ACTION NOW

ITEMS FOR ACTION NOW